# Pre-Handwriting Practice

## A Complete "First" Handwriting Program for Young and Special Learners

by
Sherrill B. Flora

illustrated by
Janet Armbrust

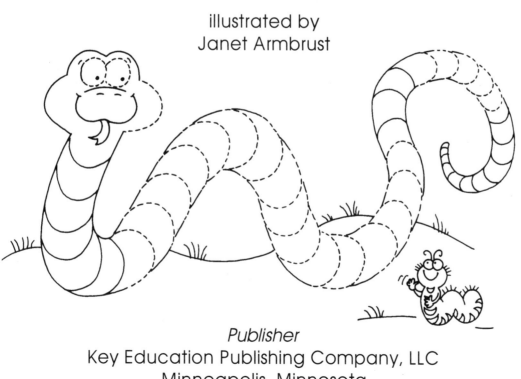

*Publisher*
Key Education Publishing Company, LLC
Minneapolis, Minnesota

## CONGRATULATIONS ON YOUR PURCHASE OF A KEY EDUCATION PRODUCT!

The editors at Key Education are former teachers who bring experience, enthusiasm, and quality to each and every product. Thousands of teachers have looked to the staff at Key Education for new and innovative resources to make their work more enjoyable and rewarding. Key Education is committed to developing educational materials that will assist teachers in building a strong and developmentally appropriate curriculum for young children.

### PLAN FOR GREAT TEACHING EXPERIENCES WHEN YOU USE
### EDUCATIONAL MATERIALS FROM KEY EDUCATION PUBLISHING COMPANY, LLC

**Standards Correlation for Pre-Handwriting Practice**
**A Complete "First" Handwriting Program for Young and Special Learners**

This book supports the NCTE/IRA Standards for the English Language Arts and the recommended teaching practices outlined in the NAEYC/IRA position statement Learning to Read and Write: Developmentally Appropriate Practices for Young Children

**NCTE/IRA Standards for the English Language Arts**

**Each activity in this book supports one or more of the following standards:**
1.  **Students communicate in spoken, written, and visual form, for a variety of purposes and a variety of audiences.** In *Pre-Handwriting Practice*, students communicate in visual and written form, by drawing lines and printing letters, to illustrate their progress in learning to write.

**NAEYC/IRA Position Statement Learning to Read and Write: Developmentally Appropriate Practices for Young Children**

**Each activity in this book supports one or more of the following recommended teaching practices for kindergarten and primary students:**
1.  **Teachers provide opportunities for students to write many different kinds of texts for different purposes.** *Pre-Handwriting Practice* includes opportunities for students to practice printing letters in order to improve their handwriting skills.

2.  **Teachers provide writing experiences that allow children to develop from the use of nonconventional writing forms to the use of more conventional forms.** In *Pre-Handwriting Practice*, students practice proper letter formation, which allows them to move toward conventional penmanship.

**Credits**
Author: Sherrill B. Flora
Inside illustrations: Janet Armbrust
Cover design: Mary Claire
Production: Key Education Staff
Editor: George C. Flora
Cover Photography: © Dyanmic Graphics

Key Education welcomes manuscripts and
product ideas from teachers.
For a copy of our submission guidelines,
please send a self-addressed, stamped envelope to:
**Key Education Publishing Company, LLC**
**Acquisitions Department**
**9601 Newton Avenue South**
**Minneapolis, Minnesota 55431**

ISBN:1-933052-02-3
*Pre-Handwriting Practice*
Copyright © 2005 by Key Education Publishing Company, LLC
Minneapolis, Minnesota 55431

# Contents

## SEQUENCE OF WHEN LETTERS ARE INTRODUCED

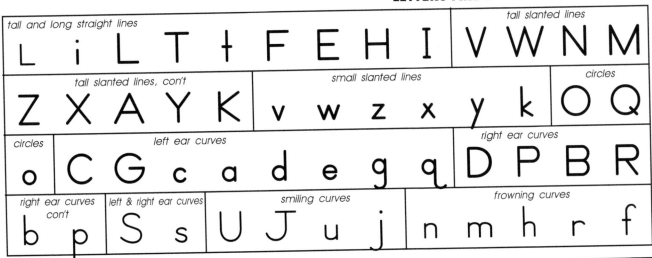

# Introduction

Learning how to print can either be a frustrating and challenging experience for a young child, or it can be a fun and successful experience. All the activities in *Pre-Handwriting Practice* have been designed to make learning how to print a successful experience.

So, what makes the difference? Often, teachers and parents present learning how to print letters in alphabetical sequence. Developmentally, this makes very little sense. Children need to learn how to control a pencil and how to make various handwriting strokes before they are able to print letters. *Pre-Handwriting Practice* gives children the opportunity to learn how to control a pencil and then learn specific handwriting strokes, which then enables them to print a variety of alphabet letters.

First, children are taught how to make "tall straight lines" and then "long straight lines." When children are able to print these lines they are then able to print "l, i, L, t, T, F, E, H, and I. Children immediately feel successful and are learning correct handwriting skills.

The strokes taught in *Pre-Handwriting Practice* are as follows:

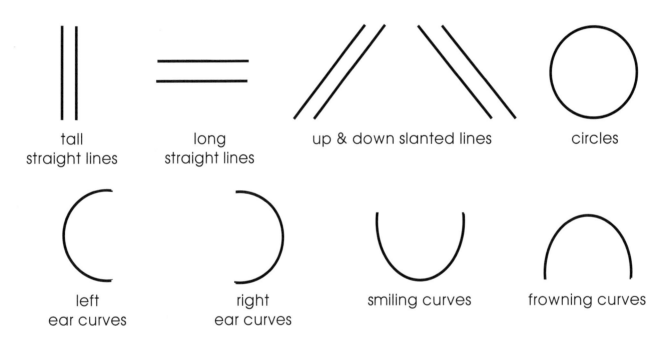

| | | | |
|---|---|---|---|
| tall straight lines | long straight lines | up & down slanted lines | circles |
| left ear curves | right ear curves | smiling curves | frowning curves |

### DIRECTIONS FOR THE TOUCH AND TRACE LETTERS

To aid in the developmental process of learning how to print, use the "Touch and Trace" cards found on pages 56–64. Reproduce these cards onto card stock and cut out along the dotted lines. Trace over each letter with glitter glue, puff paint, or a craft glue. Allow to dry. The children will be able to trace over the letters with their fingers and "feel" how each letter is formed. This tactile sensation will help imprint the correct direction of each letter, and help the child remember the proper strokes. **Use a touch and trace letter before each individual letter is introduced.** Have each of the children make their own set of "Touch and Trace" letter cards to take home for additional practice.

### EXTRA IDEAS TO STRENGTHEN FINE MOTOR SKILLS

Children need a large variety of experiences to strengthen fine motor skills and to learn how to print. Finger painting, modeling with play dough, opening and closing clothes pins, using scissors and snipping the edges of paper, peg boards, and beading are all wonderful activities that will build small muscle strength and coordination.

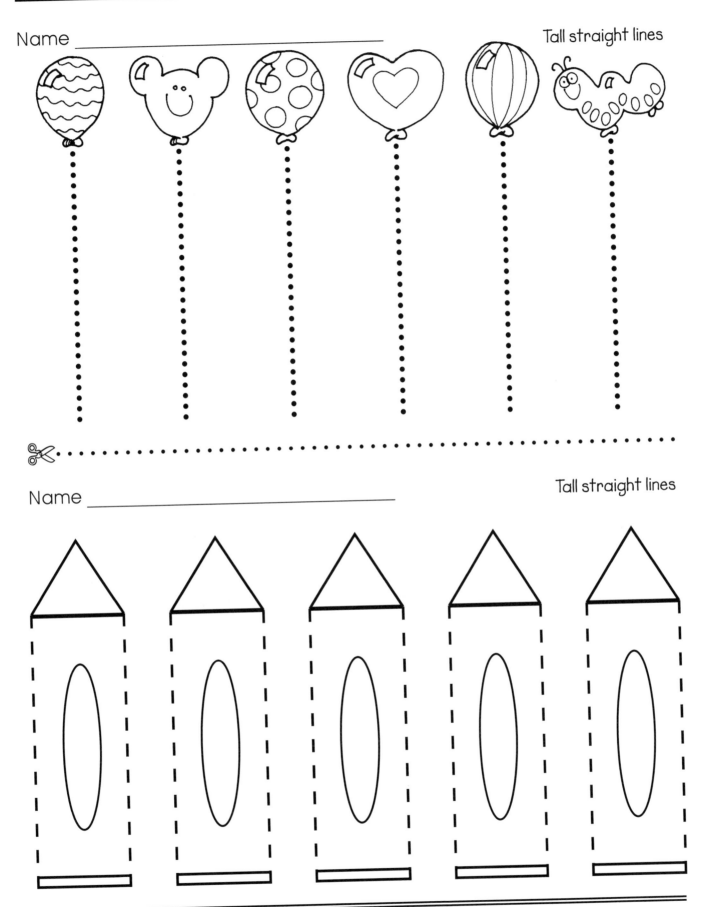

Name _____                                    Tall straight lines

Tall straight lines

Name _____

Name _____ Tall straight lines

Name _____ Tall straight lines

Name _____

Trace.

I I I I I I I I

Print all by yourself.

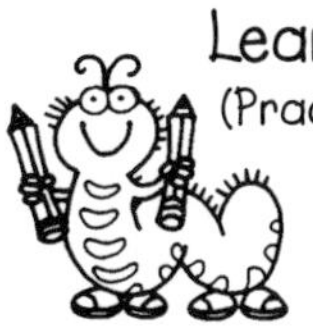

I

Name _____

Trace.

i i i i i i i i i

Print all by yourself.

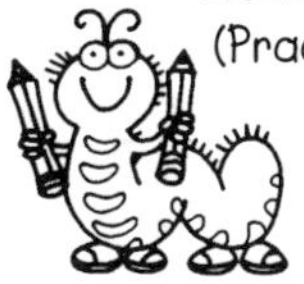

i

Name _____ Long straight lines

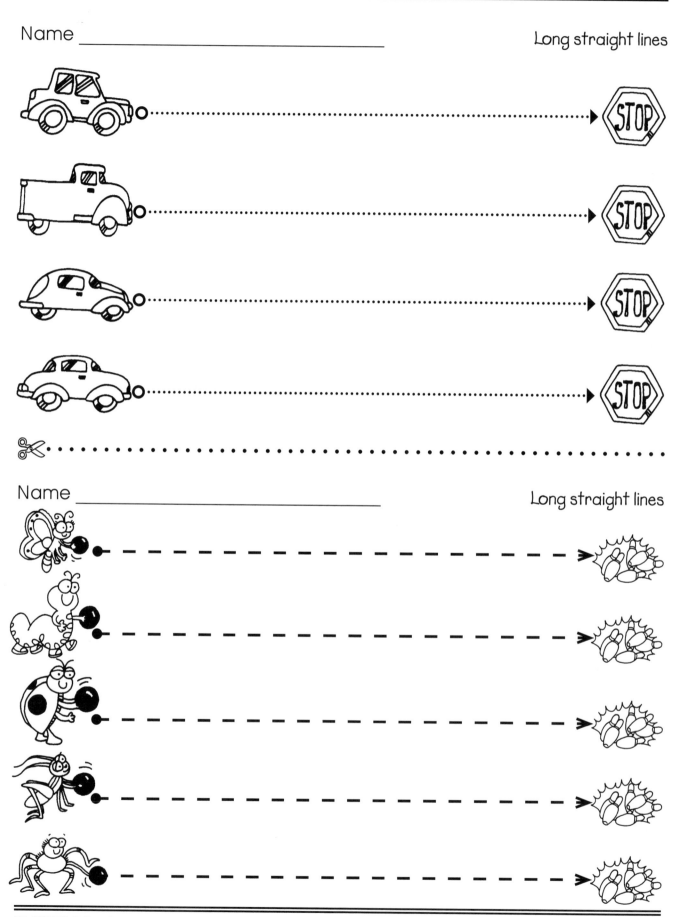

Name _____ Long straight lines

8 Pre-Handwriting Practice

Name _____  Long straight lines

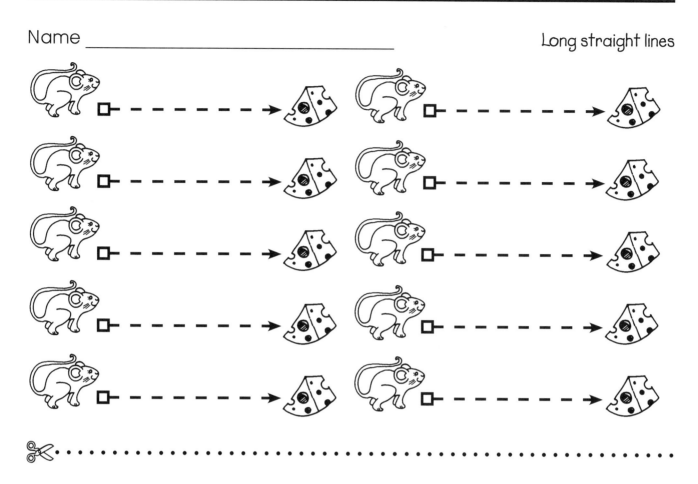

✂ • • • • • • • • • • • • • • • • • • • • • • • • • • • • • • • • • • • • • • • • • • • •

Name _____  Long straight lines

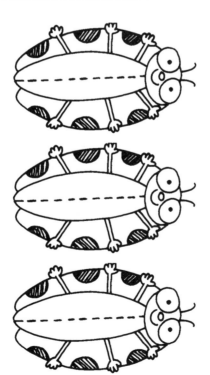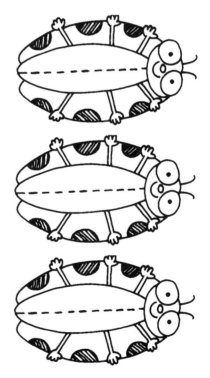

Name _____

Trace.

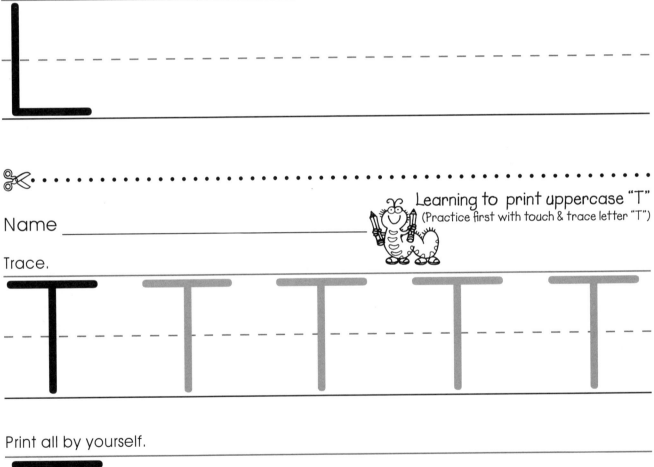

Print all by yourself.

✂ • • • • • • • • • • • • • • • • • • • • • • • • • • • • • • • • • • • • • • • • •

Name _____

Trace.

Print all by yourself.

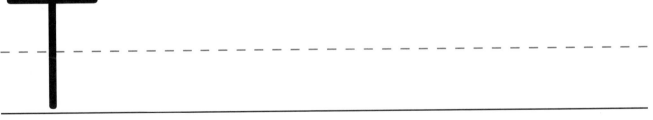

Name _____

# Review of straight lines

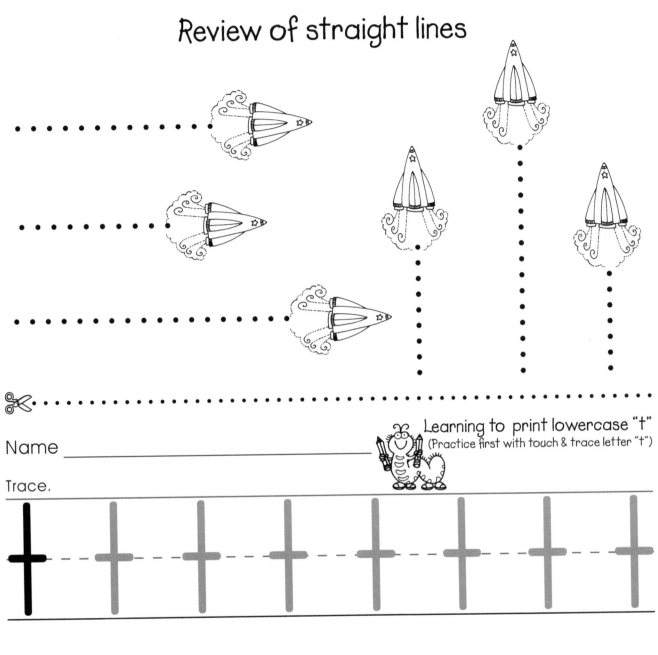

Name _____

**Learning to print lowercase "t"**
(Practice first with touch & trace letter "t")

Trace.

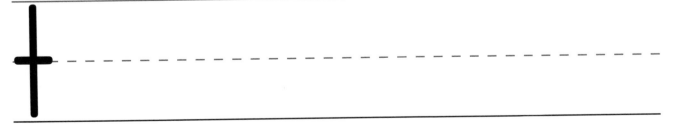

Print all by yourself.

Name _____

Trace.

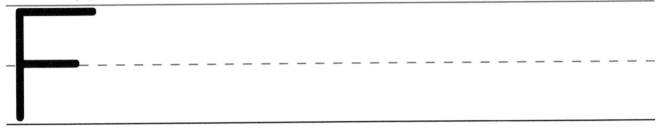

Print all by yourself.

Name _____

Trace.

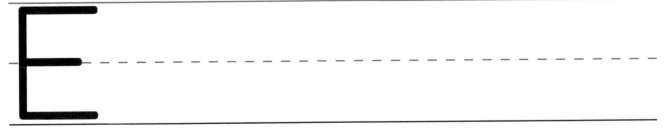

Print all by yourself.

Name _____

Trace.

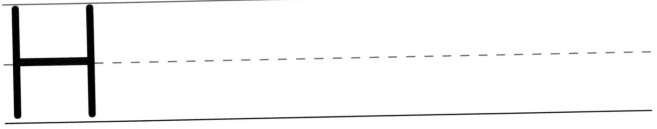

Print all by yourself.

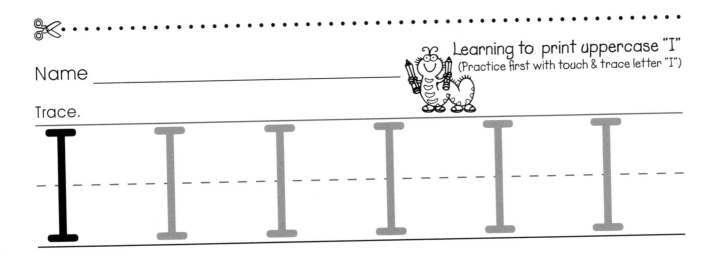

Name _____

Trace.

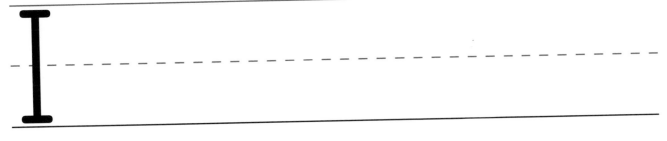

Print all by yourself.

Name _____

Name _____

Down slanted lines

Name _____                                    Up slanted lines

Name _____

Learning to print uppercase "V"
(Practice first with touch & trace letter "V")

Trace.

V V V V V

Print all by yourself.

V

Name _____

Learning to print uppercase "W"
(Practice first with touch & trace letter "W")

Trace.

W W W W W

Print all by yourself.

W

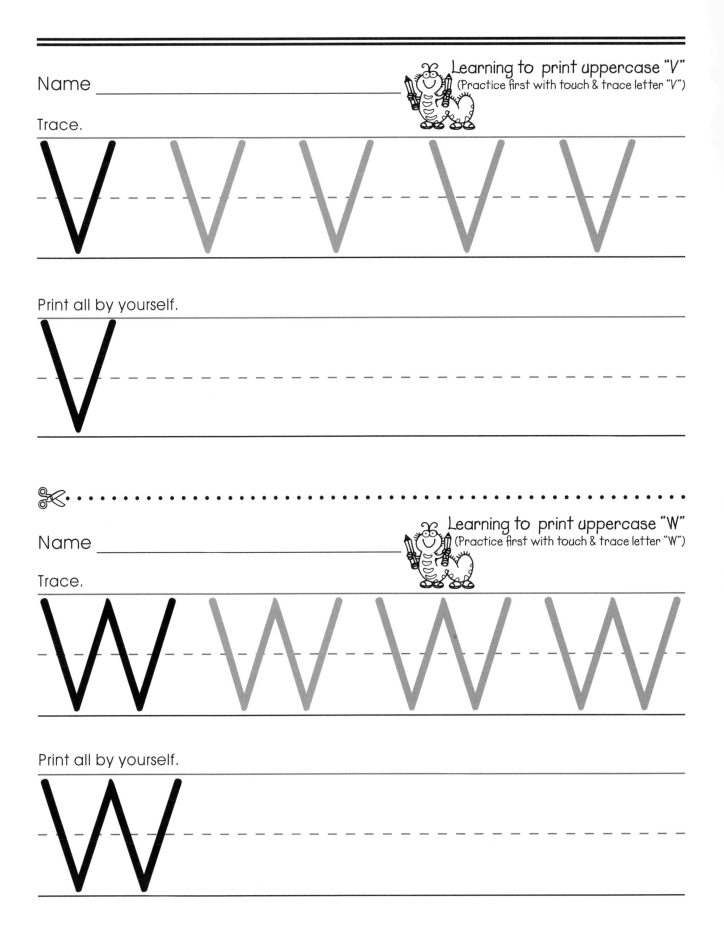

Name _____

Trace.

Print all by yourself.

N

Name _____

Trace.

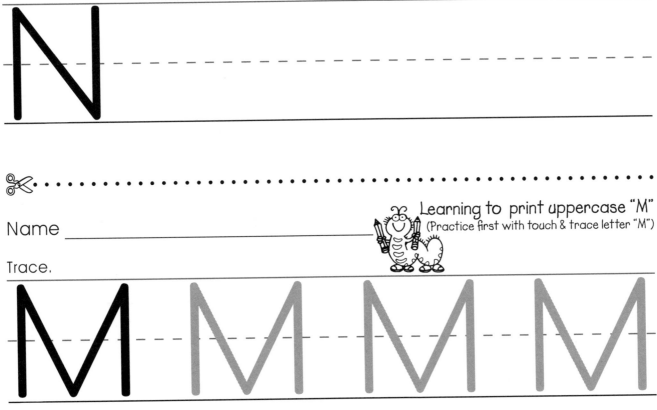

Print all by yourself.

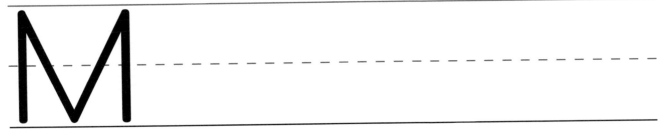

# A Walk Through the Forest
Trace tall, long, and slanted lines.

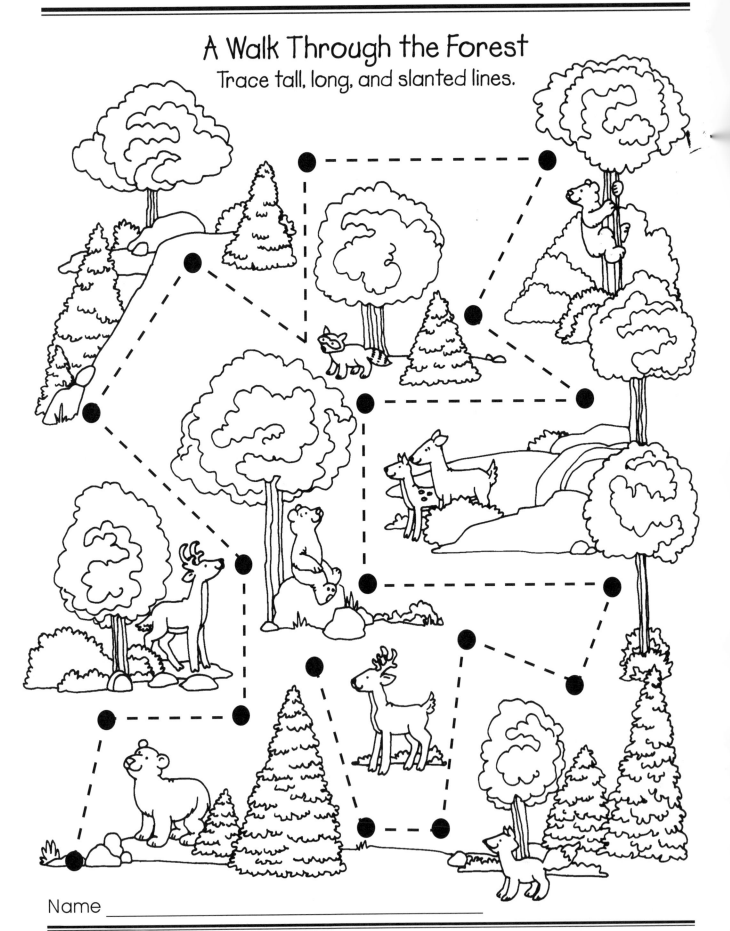

Name _____

Name _____

Learning to print uppercase "Z"
(Practice first with touch & trace letter "Z")

Trace.

Z Z Z Z Z

Print all by yourself.

Z

✂ • • • • • • • • • • • • • • • • • • • • • • • • • • • • • • • • • • •

Name _____

Learning to print uppercase "X"
(Practice first with touch & trace letter "X")

Trace.

X X X X X

Print all by yourself.

X

Name _____

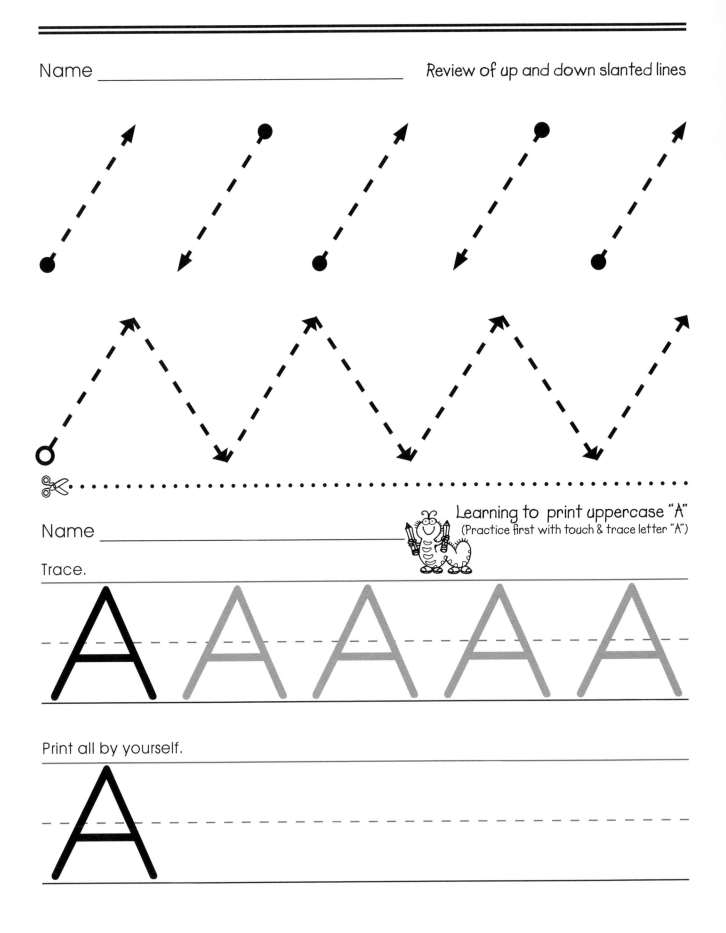

Name _____

Learning to print uppercase "A"
(Practice first with touch & trace letter "A")

Trace.

A A A A A

Print all by yourself.

A

Name _____

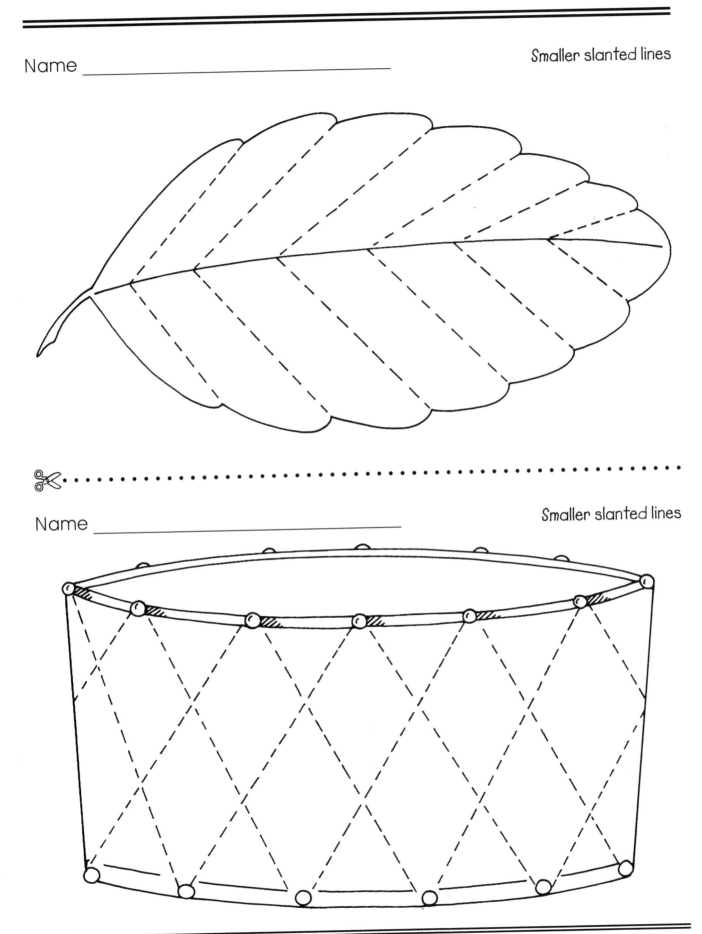

Name _____

21

Name _____

Trace.

Y Y Y Y Y

Print all by yourself.

Y

✂ • • • • • • • • • • • • • • • • • • • • • • • • • • • • • • • • • • • • • • • • • • • • • • • • • • •

Name _____

Learning to print uppercase "K"
(Practice first with touch & trace letter "K")

Trace.

K K K K K

Print all by yourself.

K

                                       Pre-Handwriting Practice

# Find the Buried Treasure
## Trace tall, long, and slanted lines.

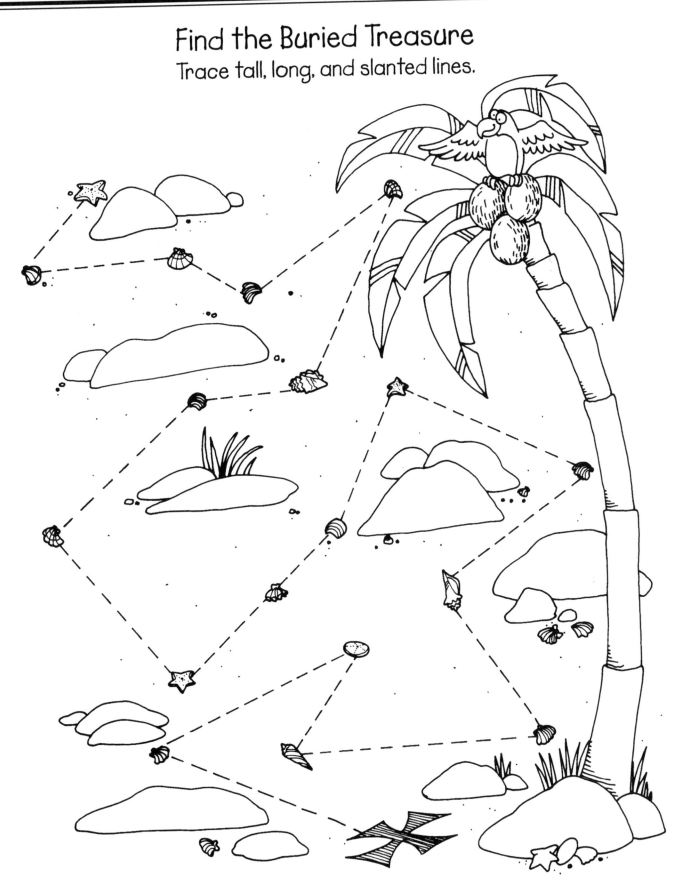

Name _____

Name _____

Trace.

V V V V V V V V

Print all by yourself.

V

Name _____

Trace.

W W W W W W W

Print all by yourself.

W

Name _____

Trace.

Z Z Z Z Z Z Z

Print all by yourself.

Z

✂ · · · · · · · · · · · · · · · · · · · · · · · · · · · · · · · · ·

Name _____

Trace.

X X X X X X X

Print all by yourself.

X

Name _____

Trace.

y y y y y y y y

y

Print all by yourself.

Name _____

Trace.

k k k k k k k

Print all by yourself.

k

✂ • • • • • • • • • • • • • • • • • • • • • • • • • • • • • • • • • • • • •

27

Name _____

Trace.

O O O O O

Print all by yourself.

O

✂ • • • • • • • • • • • • • • • • • • • • • • • • • • • • • • • •

Name _____

Trace.

Q Q Q Q Q

Print all by yourself.

Q

Name  _____

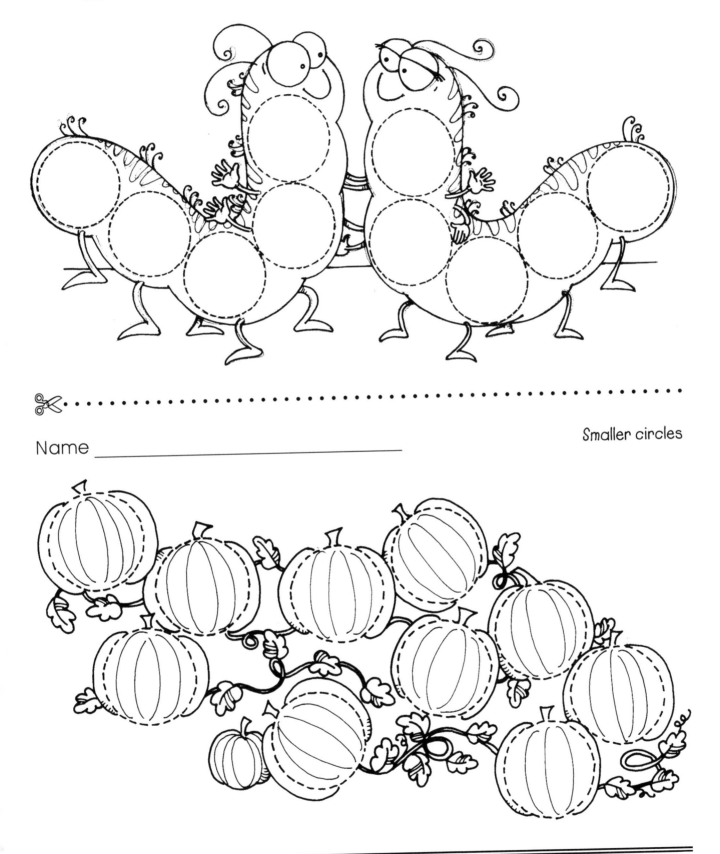

Smaller circles

Name _____

Name _____

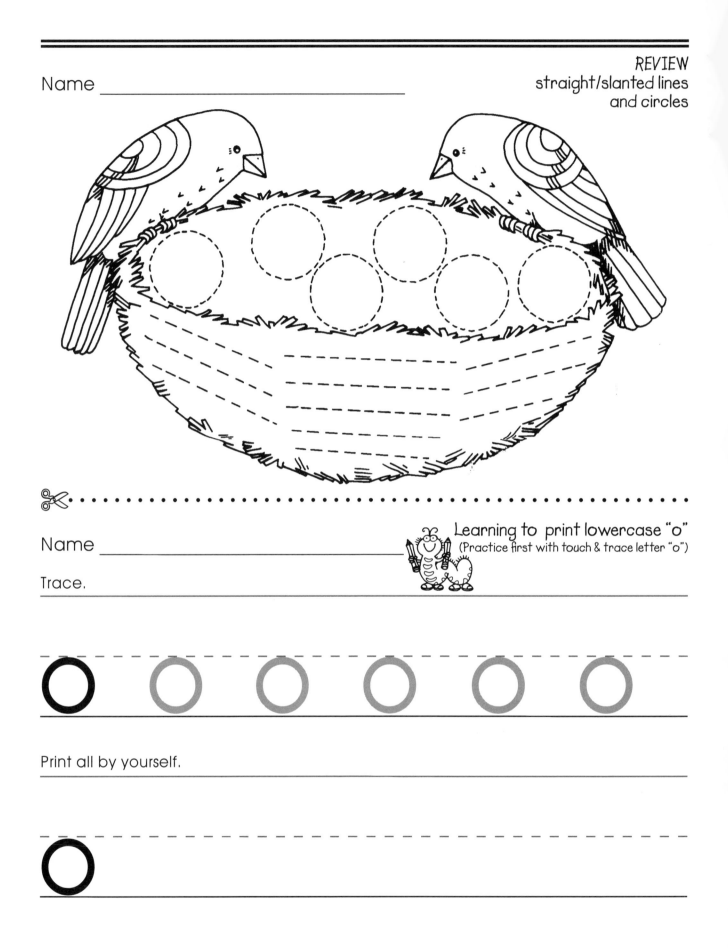

Name _____

Learning to print lowercase "o"
(Practice first with touch & trace letter "o")

Trace. _____

Print all by yourself. _____

# Up, Up, and Away!

Trace tall, long, and slanted lines and circles.

Name _____ Left ear curves

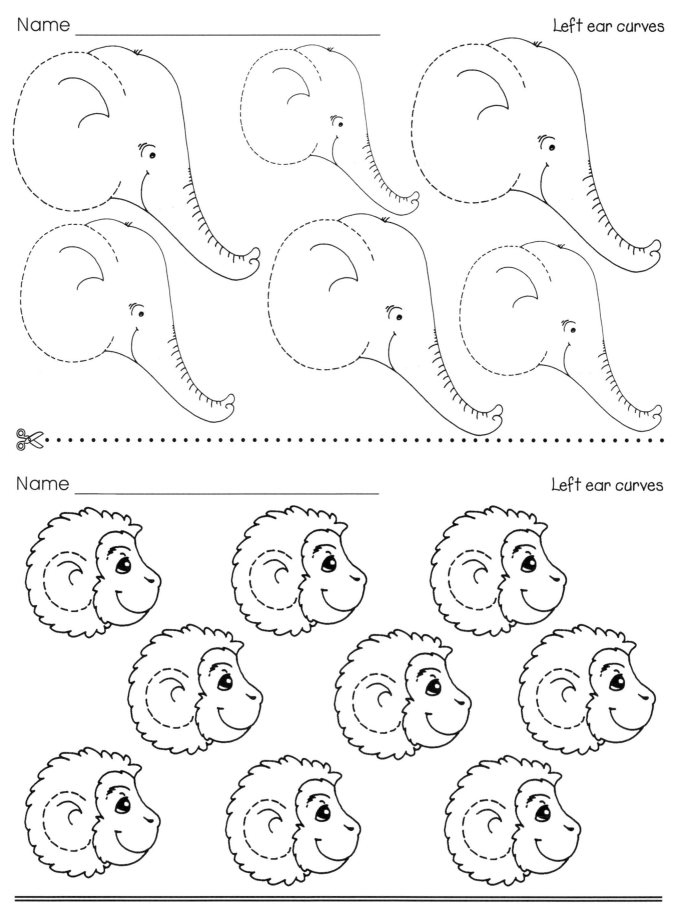

Name _____ Left ear curves

Name _____

Trace.

C C C C C

Print all by yourself.

C

✂ · · · · · · · · · · · · · · · · · · · · · · · · · · · · · · · · · ·

Learning to print uppercase "G"
(Practice first with touch & trace letter "G")

Name _____

Trace.

G G G G G

Print all by yourself.

G

Name _____

Name _____

Smaller left ear curves

Name _____

Trace. _____

c c c c c c c

Print all by yourself. _____

c

✂ • • • • • • • • • • • • • • • • • • • • • • • • • • • • • • • •

Name _____

Trace. _____

a a a a a a a

Print all by yourself. _____

a

Name _____

Trace.

d d d d d d d

Print all by yourself.

d

✂ ·············································

Name _____

Learning to print lowercase "e"
(Practice first with touch & trace letter "e")

Trace.

e e e e e e e

Print all by yourself.

e

Name _____

Trace. _____

g g g g g g g

g _____

Print all by yourself.

✂ · · · · · · · · · · · · · · · · · · · · · · · · · · · · · · · · · · · · · · · · · ·

Name _____

Learning to print lowercase "q"
(Practice first with touch & trace letter "q")

Trace. _____

q q q q q q q

q _____

Print all by yourself.

q

Name _____

Name _____

Right ear curves

38

*Pre-Handwriting Practice*

Name _____

✂ ··················································································

Name _____

**Learning to print uppercase "D"**
(Practice first with touch & trace letter "D")

Trace.

D D D D D

Print all by yourself.

D

Name _____

Name _____

Smaller right ear curves

Name _____

Learning to print uppercase "P"
(Practice first with touch & trace letter "P")

Trace.

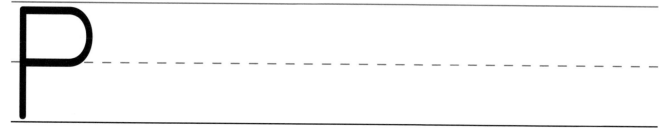

P P P P P P P

Print all by yourself.

P

Name _____

Trace.

B B B B B

Print all by yourself.

B

✂ · · · · · · · · · · · · · · · · · · · · · · · · · · · · · · · · · · · · ·

Name _____

Trace.

R R R R R

Print all by yourself.

R

Name _____

Trace.

b b b b b b b

Print all by yourself.

b

✂ ·····································································

Name _____

Trace.

p p p p p p p

p

Print all by yourself.

Name _____

Name _____

Learning to print uppercase "S"
(Practice first with touch & trace letter "S")

Trace.

S S S S S S

Print all by yourself.

S

Name _____

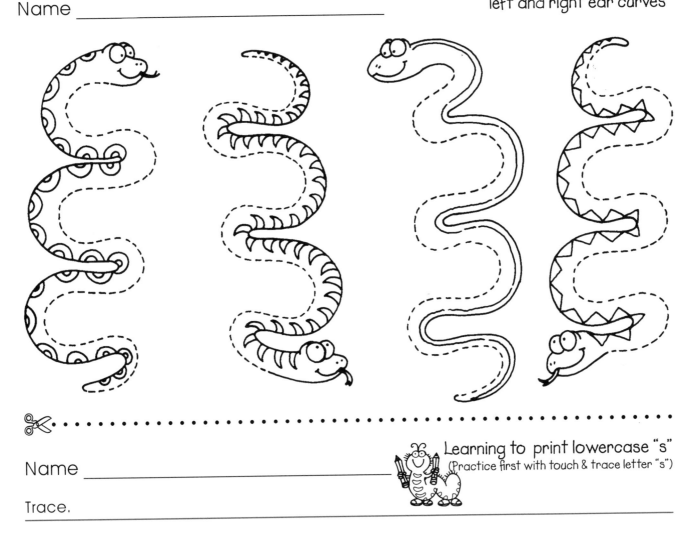

✂ · · · · · · · · · · · · · · · · · · · · · · · · · · · · · · · · · · · · · · · · · · · · ·

Name _____

Learning to print lowercase "s"
(Practice first with touch & trace letter "s")

Trace. _____

Print all by yourself.

_____

S _____

45

# Review
### Tracing long, tall, and slanted lines, circles and curves.

Name _____

Name _____          Smile curves

Name _____          Smile curves

Name _____

Trace.

U U U U U U

Print all by yourself.

U

✂ · · · · · · · · · · · · · · · · · · · · · · · · · · · · · · · · · · · · ·

Name _____

Trace.

J J J J J J

Print all by yourself.

J

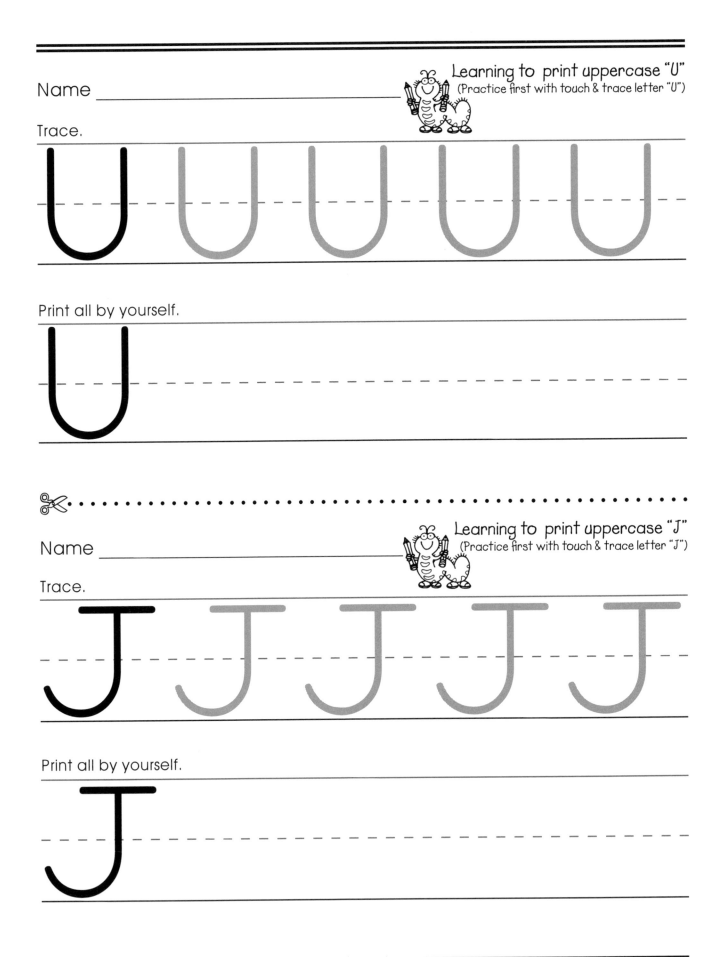

Name _____   *Smaller smile curves*

✂ · · · · · · · · · · · · · · · · · · · · · · · · · · · · · · · · · · · · · · · · · · · · ·

Name _____   *Smaller smile curves*

Trace.

u u u u u u u

Print all by yourself.

u

✂ • • • • • • • • • • • • • • • • • • • • • • • • • • • • • • • • •

Name _____

Learning to print lowercase "j"
(Practice first with touch & trace letter "j")

Trace.

j j j j j j j

j

Print all by yourself.

j

Name _____

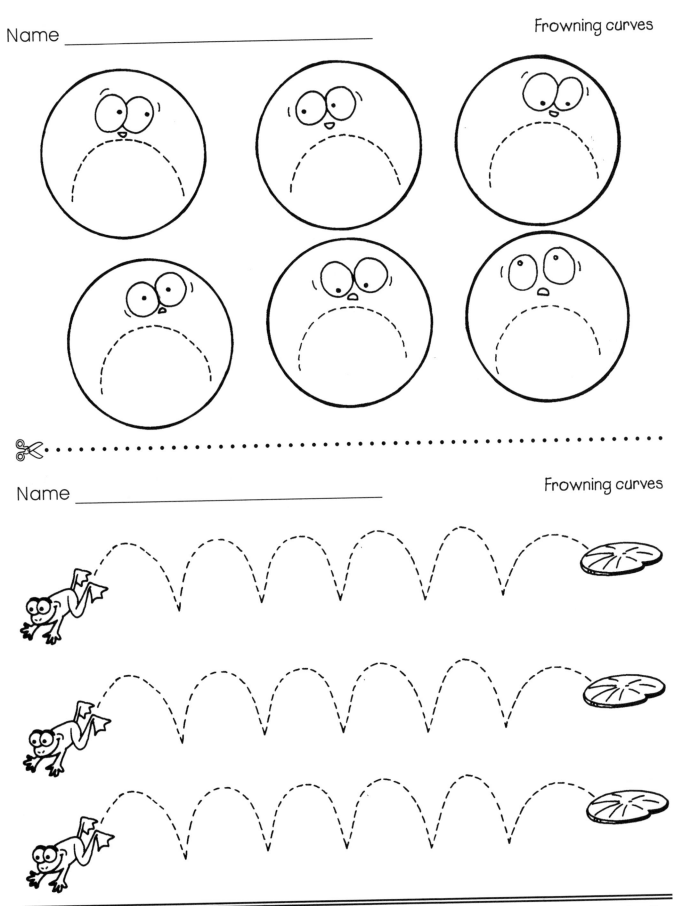

Name _____

Name _____

Trace.

n n n n n n

Print all by yourself.

n

✂ •••••••••••••••••••••••••••••••••••••••••••

Name _____

Trace.

m m m m m m

Print all by yourself.

m

Name _____

Learning to print lowercase "h"
(Practice first with touch & trace letter "h")

Trace.

h h h h h h h

Print all by yourself.

h

✂ • • • • • • • • • • • • • • • • • • • • • • • • • • • • • • • • • • • • • • • •

Name _____

Learning to print lowercase "r"
(Practice first with touch & trace letter "r")

Trace.

r r r r r r r r

Print all by yourself.

r

Name _____

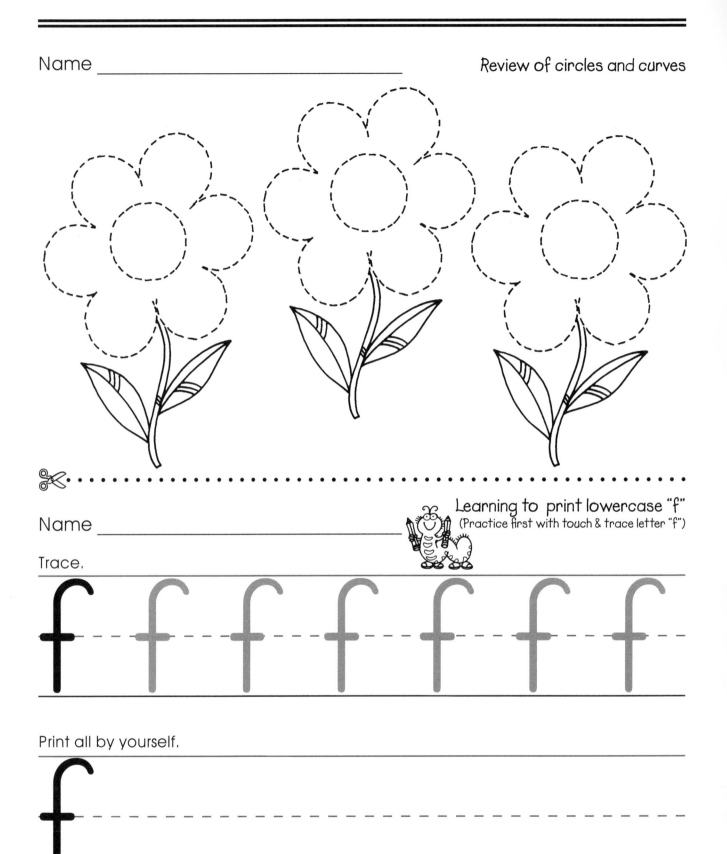

✂ • • • • • • • • • • • • • • • • • • • • • • • • • • • • • • • • • • • • • • • • • • • • • • • •

Name _____    **Learning to print lowercase "f"**
(Practice first with touch & trace letter "f")

Trace.

f f f f f f f

Print all by yourself.

f

# Fun Final Review

Name _____

## TOUCH AND TRACE LETTER DIRECTONS

To aid in the developmental process of learning how to print, use the "Touch and Trace" cards found on pages 56–64. Reproduce these cards onto card stock and cut out along the dotted lines. Trace over each letter with glitter glue, puff paint, or a craft glue. Allow to dry. The children will be able to trace over the letters with their fingers and "feel" how each letter is formed. This tactile sensation will help imprint the correct direction of each letter and help the child remember the proper strokes. Use a touch and trace letter before each individual letter is introduced. Have each of the children make their own set of "Touch and Trace" letter cards to take home for additional practice.

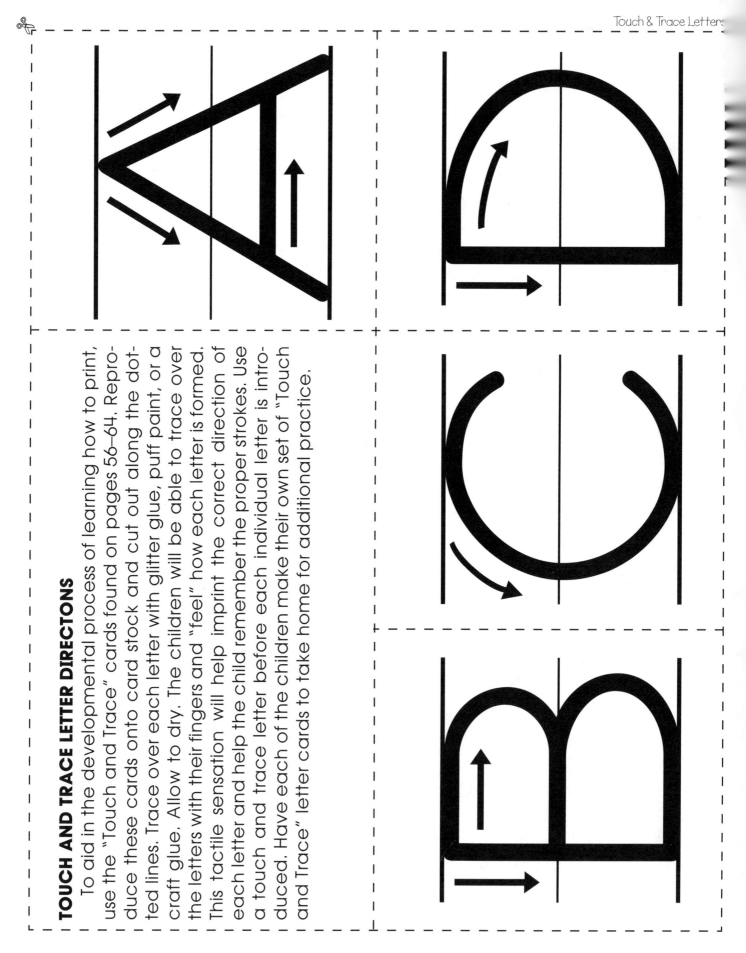

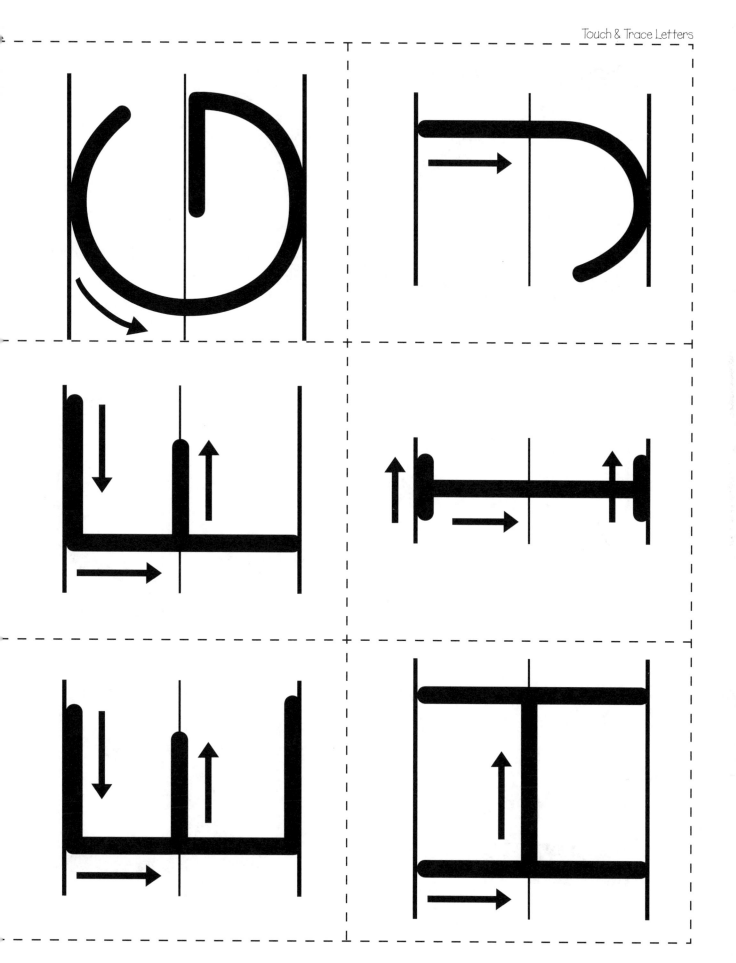

*Pre-Handwriting Practice*

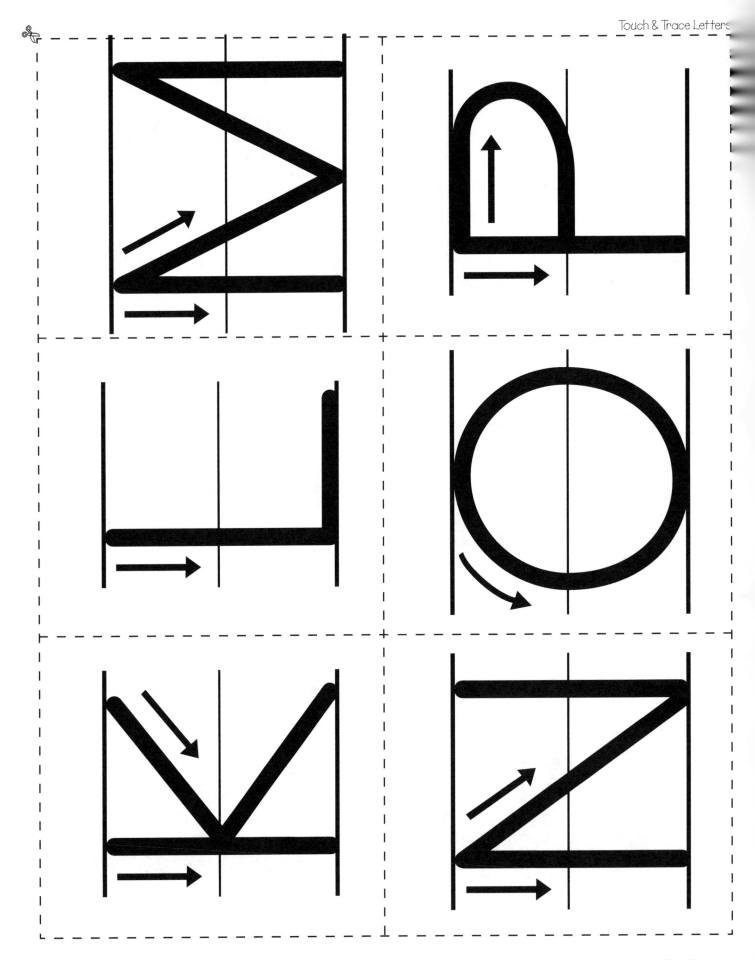

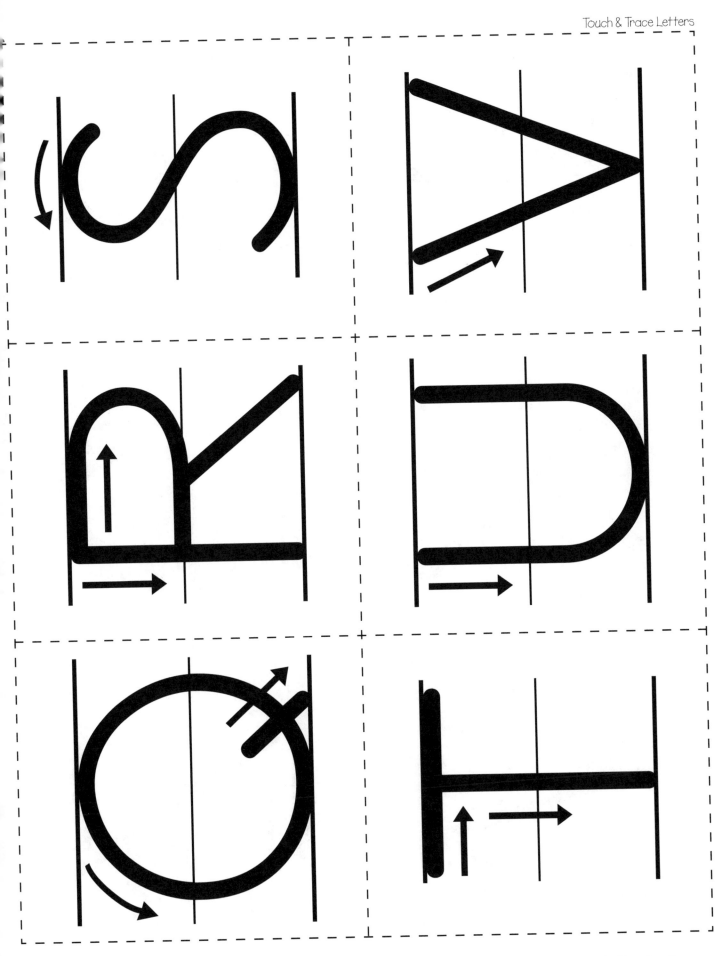

59

*Pre-Handwriting Practice*

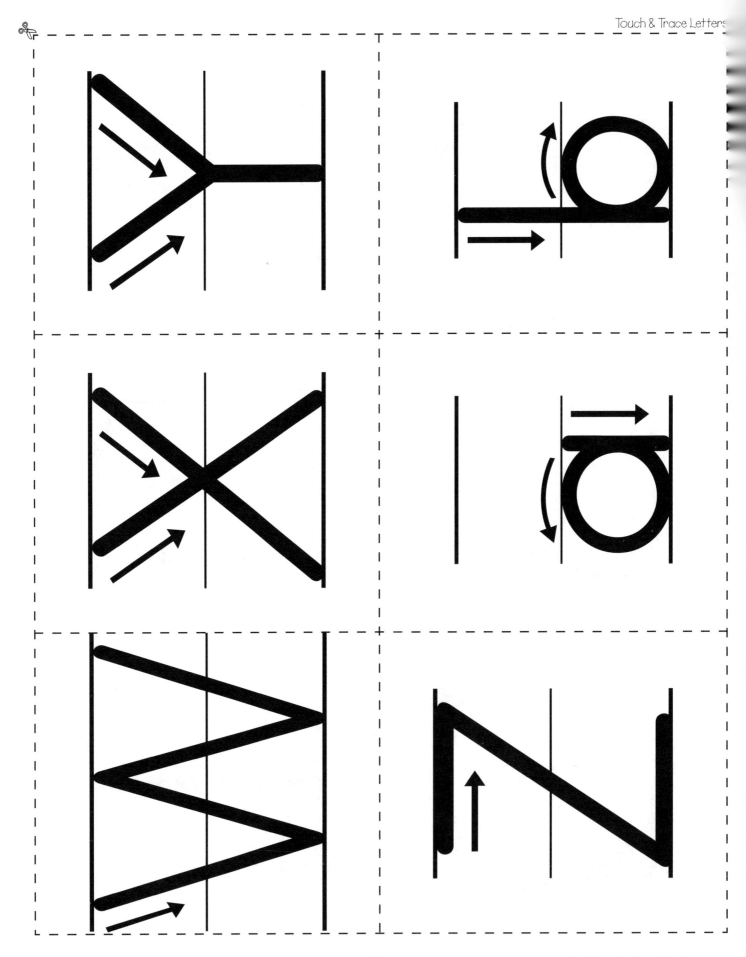

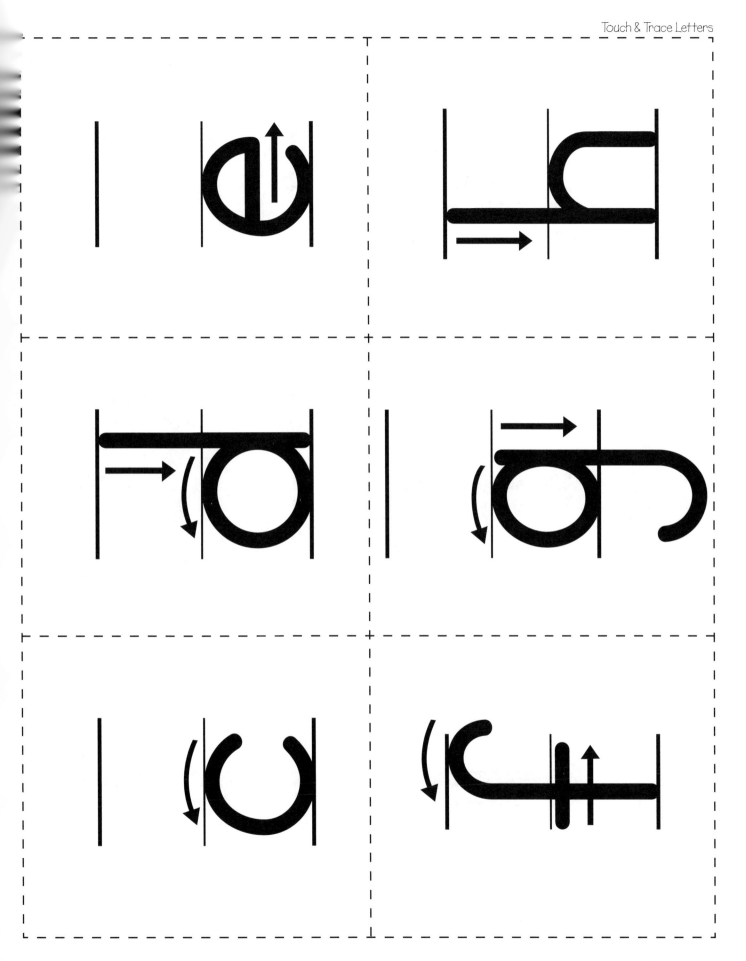

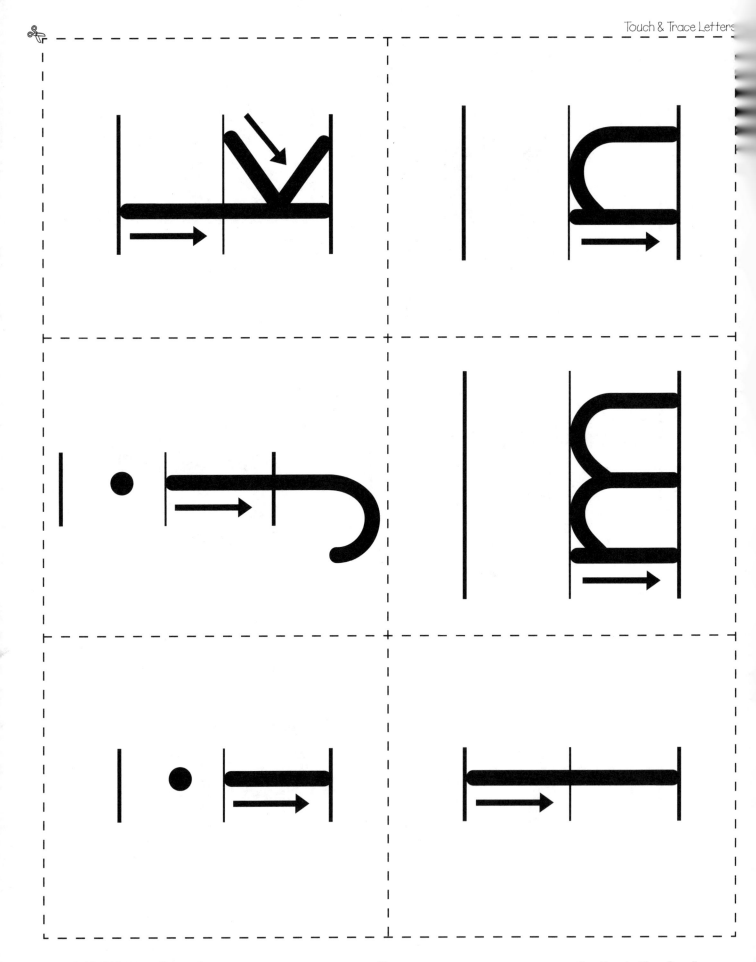

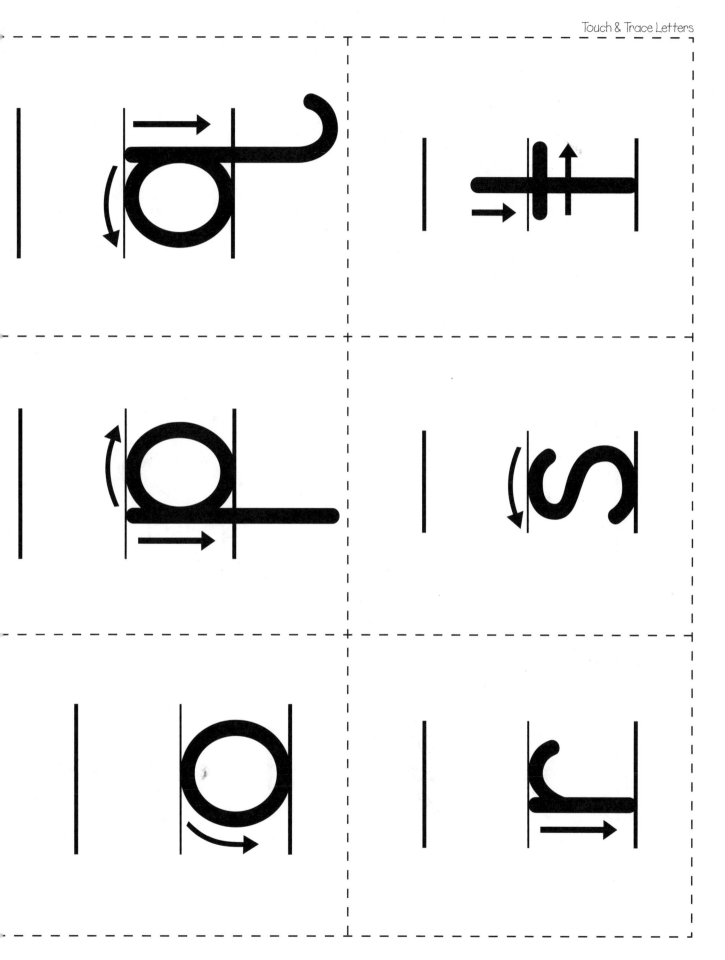

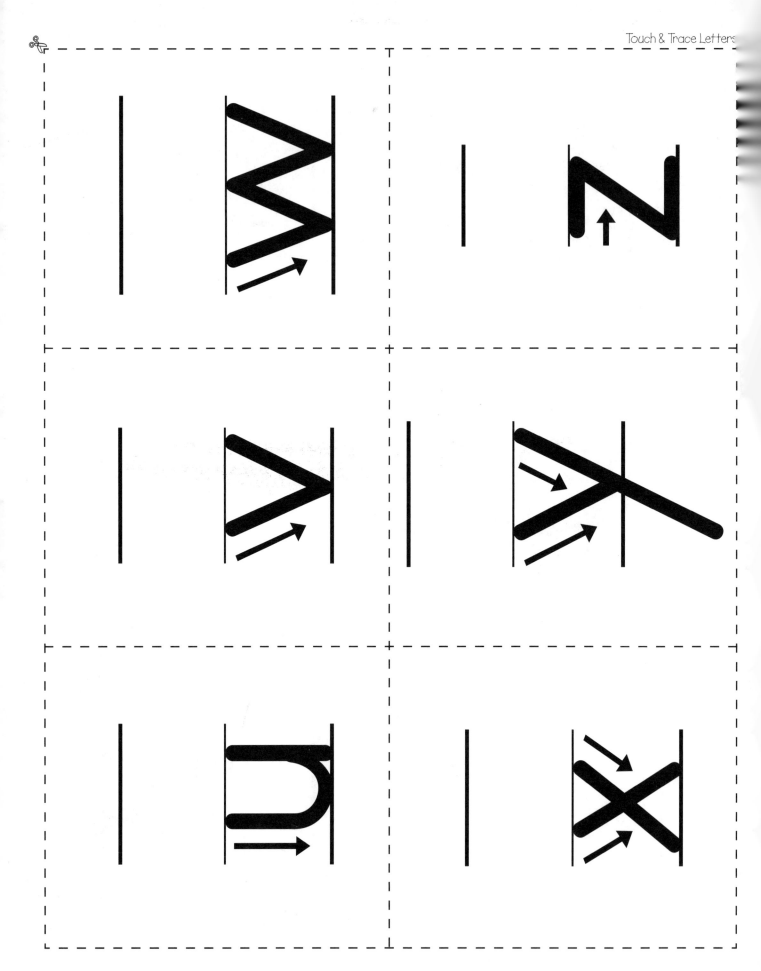